A SECOND LOOK

Gerhard E. Frost

WINSTON PRESS

Cover design: Nancy Condon

Photo credits: Nancy Bundt—cover; Cheryl Walsh Bellville—pp. 24, 47; Jean-Claude Lejeune—pp. 53, 68, 80, 85; James L. Shaffer—pp. 2, 12.

Scripture quotations in this publication are from the *Revised Standard Version Common Bible,* copyright © 1973 by the Division of Christian Education of the National Council of the Churches of Christ in the U.S.A. Used by permission.

The following selections have previously appeared in *Parish Teacher:* "The Music of the Mind," "The First Book," "Highway Reverie" (now retitled "Whose Dream Am I?"), "The Key," and "Who Did It for Me?" *The Lutheran Standard* has published "My Bush Burned," and *Scope* has published "Now I Think I Know."

Copyright © 1985 by Gerhard E. Frost.
All rights reserved. No part of this book may be reproduced in any form without written permission from Winston Press, Inc.

Library of Congress Catalog Card Number: 84-51614

ISBN: 0-86683-935-6

Printed in the United States of America

5 4 3 2 1

Winston Press, Inc.
430 Oak Grove
Minneapolis, Minnesota 55403

CONTENTS

Preface   vi
Whose Dream Am I?   1
Only Visiting   3
Who Did It for Me?   5
Swaying Room   6
Family Talk   7
Just for Me   9
Wise Counsel   10
My Dream   11
Make Me More Impulsive   11
As You Journey   13
Don't Laugh   13
"I've Missed You"   14
Everything Is Different   15
Inner Light   16
Voices   17
Is This Not Strength?   18
Making Love   19
Our Hometown   19
Turn Back   21
Home   22
The Beautiful Boast   23
Robbed   25
I'm Afraid   26
No Promise   26
New Hearts   27
I Needn't Travel Far   28
The Key   29
Autobiography   30
My Bush Burned   30
Pilate   32
Signals from Afar   33

Thank You   33
I Just Can't Understand   34
We Forget   35
The Music of the Mind   35
We Cherish for You   36
Wonderful   38
The Source Is Always Full   38
Brother John   39
Trust Him   40
Years Are Kettles   41
I've Begun Asking   42
Amazing Grace   43
I'm Right Here!   44
Easter Bread   45
Back to Earth   46
I'm the One   48
He Is No Fool   49
Joker   49
Rabbi   51
I Am Resolved   52
Young in Heart   54
Step Back   55
Wise Love   56
We Need Each Other   57
I Slammed the Door   58
Some Day We'll See   58
The First Book   59
The Halo Tilts   60
Forget-me-not   61
Just Think   62
The Question   63
Be Ready   64
Well Taught   65
Look Again   66
The Meeting   66
Now I Think I Know   69
Grounds for Hope   70

He Never Loses Touch   71
Something Beautiful   71
We Need Exits   73
To Be Continued   74
Help Us to Let Go   75
Thank You   76
My Personal Devil   76
Five Sad Words   77
The Loneliest Moment   78
What Waste!   79
Wistful   81
Two Words   81
The Talking Month   82
My Untrusting Heart   83
Pete   84
He Takes Command   84
I'm Not Super   86
Home Road   87
Those Strong Feet   88

PREFACE

I once knew a child who was fascinated with the texture and fragrance of his mother's dusting cloth. He liked to watch her graceful movements as she used it. His eager eyes followed those movements up and down the fronts and backs and legs of chairs. He liked the caressing motions of his mother as she proudly dusted her favorite pieces—tables, bookcases, and especially the piano. He was amused by the sounds as she lightly touched the keyboard from the lowest to the highest octaves and back again. Best of all, he really felt and smelled the restored "newness" of the home. I was that child.

Today as I observe my own life and the lives of others, I feel that something like that dusting cloth is needed. The dust of callousness and boredom threatens to hide the uniqueness of every passing moment. Dull routine overcomes expectation and surprise. Perhaps we may rescue one another through shared awareness and appreciation that will restore our capacity for wonder and amazement in the face of God's loving activity in our lives. God's world is always worthy of a second look.

This book is presented to you, my reader, out of the conviction that we have solid grounds for joy and hope. We count because God counts us. To you who read, I say, thanks for sharing.

WHOSE DREAM AM I?

I enjoy the moving picture from the highway:
mile on mile of theatre
and my own wandering mind.

Whose dream was this abandoned house?
Who laced the picture window?
Who chose the color, and when?
How old is old for a nourished dream,
a house, a home?

Who was the bride, and who the groom?
Did he carry her over the threshold?
Did they work and save and plan?
How many children played on this porch
when it was new?

My journey's over, and I'm home again.
I stand before the mirror.
Whose dream am I?
Who thought my life when it began?
Who shaped me in my mother's womb?
Who gives the years?
Who makes the days
and fills the moments?
Who holds the future?
Who says, "Enough"?

I hear his voice. He speaks to me:
"I don't abandon, for my dream
is you."

ONLY VISITING

Five in the morning,
sunrise in Minnesota's lakeland.
At this moment the world
is burnished gold.

I wait alone at the picture window
in solitary enjoyment
of midsummer sights and sounds.
Alone? No, not alone, for he is here,
the little half-grown chipmunk;
he's celebrating the sun,
blinking, rolling, stretching,
awakening every tiny nerve and muscle,
readying himself for the new day.

And she is here, the summer warbler,
and the hummingbirds,
both master and mistress.
Alone? No, never.
More eyes than I can count are on me
as I sit quietly.

One and all they look me over,
citizens of this diverse community,
startled, surprised, curious,
and just a bit indignant.
They make me quite defensive.

"You, trespassing again?" they seem to say.
"I thought I owned this land," is my
 embarrassed answer.
"I hold the title. I've paid!"
But it's not clear to them—or me.
These are the rightful owners. They live here.
I don't belong. I'm only visiting. I'm the
 intruder;
my deed is dated; theirs is dateless and
 supreme.

What is ownership among us mortals, anyway?

WHO DID IT FOR ME?

Journal entry, after a near tragedy:
"Thank you, God, for little children,
beagle pups, good brakes, and quick reflexes."

There he was, that puppy, on Como Avenue,
waddling unsteadily between parked cars,
and there they were, two single-minded
    children,
intent on one thing only—rescue.

As I review the swift movement
of that happy-ending plot, I think:
Who did this for me, and who for mine?
When sudden crisis drove us on and made us
    forget,
who covered for our innocence and folly?

And who stands guard today
between our children
and all that threatens
these defenseless ones?
Whose inner reflexes turn toward God
and all that's true and strong and good?
Whose anger rises in sturdy indignation,
lets love's eyes flash
on behalf of all the threatened ones?

SWAYING ROOM

Today I have been tutored
by the forest in its wisdom.

One week ago I cut some aspens into post
   lengths,
reverting to my farmer days.
(I'll cut them for the fireplace
some other time, I told myself.)
I placed them tip to tip around a growing
   tree.
Today that sturdy tree is broken,
shattered eight feet above the ground.

I killed the tree by forcing it
to be more rigid than any growing thing can
   be—
a thoughtless thing to do.
I should have known
that living things need swaying room;
it's also true of persons.

Yes, growing things need space,
room for changing and responding.
Brittle systems maim and kill.

FAMILY TALK

The Lord's Day,
and I, a thousand miles from home,
went to church.

I felt alone.

I knew no name,
was known by none,
or so I thought
until we rose as one,
affirming, "I believe . . .

In God," we said.
I saw it then;
I knew the Road.

We walked together.

". . . the Father Almighty . . .
Jesus Christ, . . . the Holy Spirit."
We felt the Rock beneath our feet,
felt it and were comforted.

". . . conceived by the Holy Spirit, . . .
born, . . . crucified, . . .
dead, . . . buried, . . . rose, . . .
  ascended, . . .
will come again. . . ."
We saw the Light
and shared our hope.

"The holy Christian Church, . . .
    forgiveness, . . .
resurrection, . . . life everlasting. . . .
    Amen."
I knew them by their family talk.

And we were one.

JUST FOR ME

It was the kind of day
that comes to anyone,
not my day, I thought,
not even the Lord's.

Chapel time, and I,
turned in upon myself,
bundled in defiance and discouragement,
went on my heavy-footed way.

My friend rose to bring the message.
"Message!" I thought, and dared him
to say one thing that spoke to me.
Then, with his first word, it came:
"Grace to *you*, and peace."
There it was, all I needed, just for me.
Seldom have I felt such force in words
as I did then. "Grace to *you*. . . . "
A flashback of my baptism—
grace and peace, two all-sufficient girders
for the heaviest burdens life can lay on
   anyone.
Even as I recall them on this distant day
I feel healed, supported, and sustained.

WISE COUNSEL

The subject was snakes,
and no one in fourth-grade
nature class was bored.
They spoke of many snake affairs:
their homes, their habits, their uses.
But they spoke of dangers, too,
and when the teacher's question came:
"What should you do if you come
suddenly upon a snake?"
one thoughtful child responded,
"Walk backwards, slowly."

Wise counsel. Show care and courage in
   retreating.
Absent yourself. Don't panic,
but have nothing to do with the creature
if you're not sure.

In life's journey, too,
there are times to walk backwards, slowly.
We can avoid many regrets
if we have courage to retreat.

MY DREAM

This was my dream:
I'd just arrived within The Gates,
approached the throne, and boldly asked:
"Tell me, all-wise and loving God,
what is the greatest work on earth
since the birthing and the rising of your Son?"
He smiled, then drew me to his side and said,
"My children crying 'Father!'"

MAKE ME MORE IMPULSIVE

I see red taillights, Lord,
taillights of opportunity
vanishing into the night of yesterday;
I've watched them through the years,
tormented by the Story I am
but haven't often shared:
the "little Christ" I'm called to be
but haven't always been.

I've played it oh so safe, Lord,
picked my careful, plodding course.
Make me more impulsive,
more prodigal for you. Amen.

AS YOU JOURNEY

As you journey
through your days,
don't miss the beauty
of weathered things—
rock, wood, metal, faces—
especially faces.

DON'T LAUGH

They told me today
of the chain smoker who read so much
about the hazards of smoking
that he finally decided to give up reading.
They expected me to laugh.
And I did.

But then I thought,
"What about me?"

Our Lord says,
Love one another,
love your enemies,
seek justice,
forgive as you have been forgiven.

Something in me doesn't like that.
So sometimes I read less
and less.

Don't laugh.

"I'VE MISSED YOU"

I knocked today at my friend's door;
he answered, and I went in.
"I've the best possible reason
for coming," I said.
"What's that?" said he.
"I've missed you."

I had no other reason.
I just wanted to stand up close,
shoulder to shoulder, heart to heart,
with this, my friend.
We found it reason enough.

EVERYTHING IS DIFFERENT

"And behold, angels came
and ministered to him."

Angels came.
Our Lord experienced this,
and my heart says, "Me, too!"

Nothing has changed,
yet everything is different
(don't ask me to explain):
My journey waits, my cross remains,
my wilderness retains its wildness.
But oh the difference
since angels came!

INNER LIGHT

She lives alone,
and told us this:
She sometimes lights a single candle,
and it becomes for her an inner light
and source of joy.

We talked about
why this was so.
It's such an elemental light, we said,
so living and so real,
exceeded only
by the Star.

There's warmth and welcome there.

VOICES

I saw them just today—
two bumper stickers on one bumper,
the first a scream, the second a whisper.
The one said, "Stop the arms race,
not the human race"; the other,
"Share a book with a child today."

As I think of these voices now,
they aren't two, but one;
they complement each other.
There are no quick and easy panaceas
in our divided world.
Peace and understanding move forward
only in the slow and tortuous march of truth
as she "limps along on the arm of time."

IS THIS NOT STRENGTH?

He'd been asked
to offer the invocation
for his fiftieth class reunion.

He began
but couldn't continue.
The flood of grace unbounded
choked back all words.
Feelings of unworthiness and awe
overwhelmed and silenced him.

Quickly another stepped forward
and carried on.

Later he brought an apology
for "weakness,"
but, surely, to respond honestly
to years of grace and goodness,
years with God and God's—
is this not strength?

MAKING LOVE

Making love,
the ultimate frolic,
is the art of being second;
you dare not be good to yourself
until you've been good to the other.

Nourished, and sometimes saved, by a sense of humor,
love is the horizon of all that's human,
forever beyond our grasp, never fully attained;
when you think you've arrived, it eludes you.

Indeed, it is an art,
full of significance and majesty.

OUR HOMETOWN

In my hometown,
when we had a problem,
I remember the grown-ups getting together
to share the wisdom of the village.
They knew
it wouldn't be well with any of us
unless it was well with all of us.

Today, in our hometown,
our global village,
we trust in fear
to hold things together.

Unless we come together
and practice wise cooperation,
we'll be like the six foolish people
who tried to push their car
out of the mud
by taking turns at pushing.

We need to join hands.
After all, it's our hometown.

TURN BACK

"One of them, when he saw
that he was healed, turned back,
praising God. . . ."

"I can handle it," I hear them say,
and I've said it, too.
But it's the Big Lie.

Ten lepers were healed that day;
nine thought they could handle it.
Cleansed, restored, and free,
with places to go and people to see,
and much catching up to do,
they couldn't handle it.

They lost their way.

But one gave his health to the healer;
he turned back, praising God.
He let God handle it.

HOME

Home is where you are
even when you're not;
where you unbutton whatever is pinching you,
loosen whatever is choking you,
set down whatever is breaking you,
and tell whatever is bothering you.

Home is where someone is expecting you,
where your chair, your plate,
your bed are always kept for you,
where a memory, a plan, a dream, a laugh,
or a tear is freely shared with you.

Home is where you let up and let down,
where you stop hiding and let yourself be
   found,
where you quit being someone else
and are just your needy little old self.

THE BEAUTIFUL BOAST

We need bragging rights;
without them we can't be whole.

Our Lord knows this.
What are the psalms of praise
but holy boasts,
the family or the nation
boasting of its God?

She was only three,
but her voice was strong and shrill.
I would swing her high in the public park,
and the bragging would begin:
"My granddaddy is so strong,
he swing me higher than *anybody!*"
She'd say it with a toss of her pretty head.

A bit embarrassed, I'd shush her down,
but not too much. I knew, I understood.
She needs this, I'd tell myself.
I mustn't deprive her
of her beautiful boast.

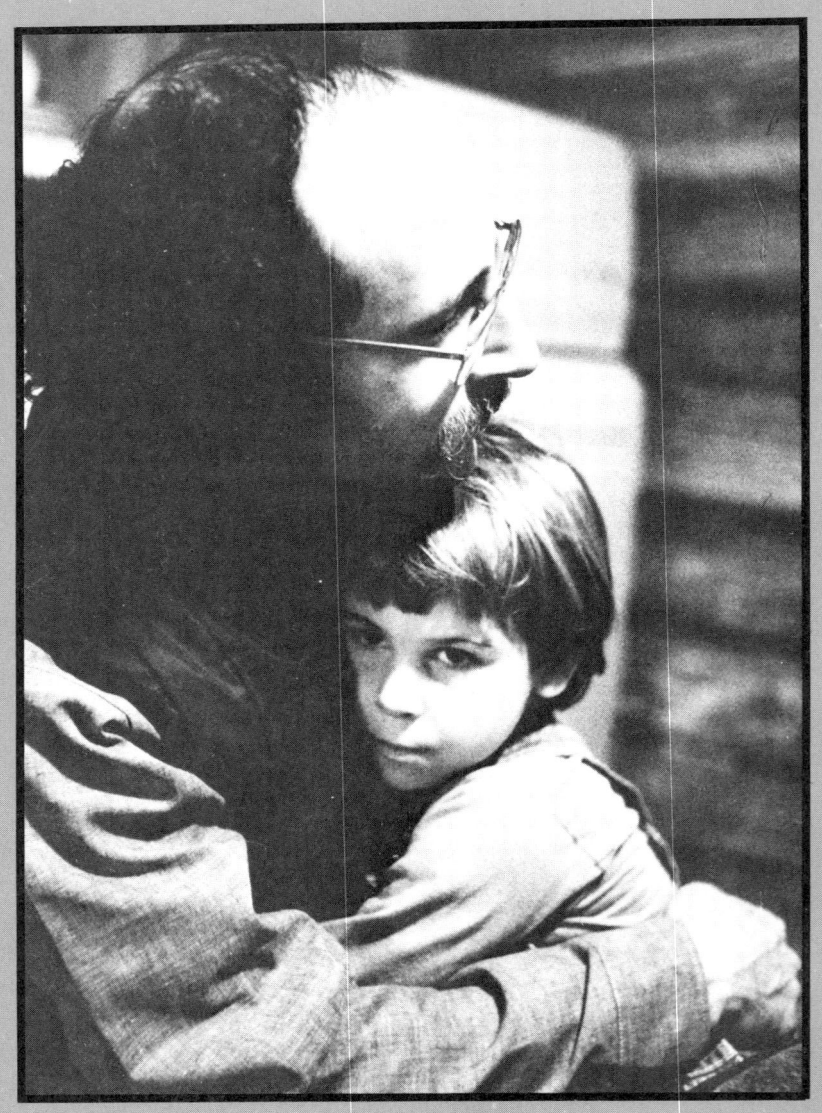

ROBBED

Little Jacob, happy child,
broke down and cried in church today,
sobbed a three-year-old's
anger and frustration
at being robbed. His reason?
They'd omitted the "Our Father,"
the very part he'd waited for,
the one he knew included and belonged to
  him.
(Oh, he doesn't really know it;
he piggybacks on those who do,
but soon he will!)

We grown-ups wonder,
Should we bring these wiggly ones?
What happens? Does Jesus really touch them?

Little Jacob teaches well:
Don't rob me of my best,
he says.

I'M AFRAID

God, I'm afraid,
afraid to pray
"Thy will be done."
I reach for a hard hat,
expect my sky to fall.
I almost hold my breath.

I know your will is more than best;
it is the only good.
Forgive my deep distrust,
the sin I've sinned
and sin again.

Remove the dark suspicion
from my heart.

NO PROMISE

Kind thoughts and good impulses
come and go, go and come,
with no promise
to return!

NEW HEARTS

"Sit here, . . . remain
. . . , and watch."

We are your activists, dear Lord,
like Peter, James, John,
and all the other nine.
We go, we do, we tell.

But please, Lord, don't speak
those hard and grown-up words:
Sit, remain, watch!
(We sleep a lot, you know.)

Or dare we ask new hearts to share
your promise and your pain?

I NEEDN'T TRAVEL FAR

They had journeyed far,
two first-time travelers,
and now had just returned
when someone mentioned Rome.

"Rome? Rome? Weren't we in Rome?"
said one to the other.
"Oh, yes!" was the reply.
"Don't you remember?
That's where we fed the pigeons."

I think of myself,
and how I limit what I'm looking at.
I pine for the unusual, but I needn't travel far.
I know this all-important truth:
Unless I see great sights at home
I'll miss them all in Rome.

THE KEY

Four years in his first parish. . . .
I remembered him as a good presence
in and out of my classroom: a seeker and
  asker,
alive and interesting,
an encourager to any teacher.

I asked him now, expecting a different
  response:
"After these years on the firing line,
what have you found to be your greatest gifts
in ministry?"

He deliberated.
I waited longer than I'd expected to.
Then his answer came, without a trace of
  flippancy:
"Well, for one thing, I'm good at holding
  babies."

Good at holding babies!
It brings back pictures,
one in particular I saw often in my childhood:
a picture of Jesus, strong Son of God, Lion of
  Judah,
in which he's holding babies.
"Let the children come," he said.

Is this the first and greatest step
toward faithful following—to be open to the young?
Is this the golden key to discipleship
for everyone?

AUTOBIOGRAPHY

If you should ask me,
"Who are you right now?
Where are you?
What road have you taken?
What have you become?"
I needn't give you fifty pages,
or even five, or one.
My check stubs are enough.

MY BUSH BURNED

My bush burned this morning,
burned and was not consumed,
as I gathered with sisters and brothers in the faith
for the ultimate act of defiance,
a Christian burial service.

My heart soared and sang
as I joined in the demonstration
and hurled the name of Jesus
into the face of the enemy,
Death.

Never have I sensed so deeply
the heaven-sent boldness
of comforting one another
"with the comfort with which we ourselves
are comforted by God"
and taking to the streets again
with other comforted ones
under the defiant benediction.

The bush still burns.

PILATE

"Pilate sent him over to Herod. . . ."

I played Pilate today,
and I'm ashamed;
didn't mean to, never planned to,
but I sent Jesus to Herod.

At the hot-potato moment,
when I was on the spot,
I said casually,
"Somebody ought to do something about
 this."
In the silence that followed
I sent Jesus to somebody else.
Now I know it was to Herod,
and I was Pilate.

Have mercy, Lord,
for when the pressure's on
I still go looking for "Herod,"
the mythical presence
named "Somebody Else."
Pilate did it. I do, too.

SIGNALS FROM AFAR

"She was so good
at bringing people together."
High praise from one tall son
at the funeral of his mother.

To be a bridge to others:
What can be more truly human?
What greater use of gifts than this,
to be a reconciler?

One thing I've noted through the years:
A bridge is almost always beautiful,
a wall hardly ever.

Two dates on every silent stone
send signals from afar:
"Be swift," they say, "and strong at building,
and let it be a bridge."

THANK YOU

O God,
I meet you in my friends
and enemies,
all the time
and everywhere.

Thank you
for living there.
Yes!

I JUST CAN'T UNDERSTAND

It had been a teachers' workshop,
and we'd talked about important things.
At closing time the subject had been mystery:
what to do with questions only God can
    answer.
Someone shared this parting thought,
a happening in her class.

They, too, had spoken of things not
    understood,
when one child, brightest and most articulate,
    said:
"Oh, I understand God! And I understand
    Jesus!
I understand heaven and how God made the
    world,
and a lot of stuff like that.
But there's one thing I just can't understand.
Chicken pox!"

A slice of life.
We pitch our tents amid the awesome and the
    wonderful;
we learn to rest on the outskirts of
    magnificence and mystery,
but little things just won't make sense,
and sometimes they tempt us to doubt
the goodness
of our God.

WE FORGET

Impressed with our thought,
we forget to stand in awe
before the fact that we're thinking.

Entranced with our being,
we forget to rejoice
in our constant becoming.

Bent on achieving,
we forget to be humbled
by God's gracious giving.

THE MUSIC OF THE MIND

We spoke of heritage,
of things worth passing on.
The talk turned toward
selective memorization:
how wise it is to stock
the cupboards of the mind
with things that feed the heart.

How strengthening, we all agreed,
in sun-bright day or darkest night
(when bushes look like bears, you know),
when health abounds or sickness weighs,
to gather all the best one knows
and play it like an organ:
Rehearse, enjoy, grow strong on this,
the music of the mind.

One sagely said, "I've found it good
to memorize at least six classic prayers
for those half dozen moods that make up most
   of life."

WE CHERISH FOR YOU
(Words at a Wedding)

We cherish for you
joy and peace in believing,
the joy of trusting
and of being trusted,
of forgiving
and of being forgiven.

We cherish for you
the enriching rhythm
of togetherness and separateness,
for unless you are at home in the "stillness,"
you cannot be God's intention
to each other.

We cherish for you
the rhythm of silence and loving speech,
for relationship is tested
by how it employs silence
and the many forms of speech.

We cherish for you
the rhythm of privacy and intimacy,
that you may not over-possess each other,
for you belonged to God
even before you knew each other.

We cherish for you
the rhythm of pain and pleasure.
We speak not now of inevitable pain,
but of the pain you choose because you care,
for "without a hurt the heart is hollow."

We look with longing after you
but run with hope before you.
In the bittersweet joy of your departing we
   pray:
God bless them unto more and more
of living and loving.

WONDERFUL

It's awesome
and wonderful
to meet a person
who knows the way Home.

THE SOURCE IS ALWAYS FULL

I'm thinking of our first,
toddling two-year-old.

I came into our living room
and found her wrestling with a heavy book of
  mine.
There she sat, slowly turning pages,
mournfully repeating, "Nussin' in 'ere!
Nussin' in 'ere!"

It was a good book
(F. W. Robertson's *Sermons!*).
But she was right:
There was nothing in there for a child—
no story, no picture, no song.

Our God, as Father, is true to himself and us;
there's always something for his child.
He speaks the language of his smallest ones,
not to explain, but to *give* himself in love.

The heart can receive
what no mind can comprehend;
the source that fills it
is always full.

BROTHER JOHN

Brother John taught us well,
taught us how to die.

That generous, helpful man—
we'd called on him so often.
And he never failed to come.

But then he died.

I'll not forget him
spending all his waning strength
in family embrace, in reaching out
to all his eight, and to his loving wife.

He knew the way of love:
to live in God's embrace.

TRUST HIM

Jesus came
not from "above" but from "below":
in a birth as a babe,
a saving event.

He came
not to play favorites
with the intellectually elite,
the grand, the few.

He came
not to be understood and explained,
but to be loved and trusted.

He came
to tell us
that in all our striving for knowledge
there is heart work to do.

YEARS ARE KETTLES

I like soup,
especially the second day:
Simmering is important.

Only simmered knowledge
has enough of living flavor
to qualify as wisdom.

Years are kettles.
They hold the goodness
of recollected joy and sadness.

People say I'm old.
That's all right with me
as long as simmering contentment
leaves its mellow residue.

I'VE BEGUN ASKING

I'm breaking my habit
of asking strangers,
"What do you do?"
as if they're no more than what they do.

I've begun asking,
"What are your dreams and your dreads?
What moves you, excites you, alarms you?
What drains you, or sustains you?
What interests or bores you, amuses or grieves
   you?
Where do you go when you're homesick?
Where do you rest when you're tired?
Who are you when you're alone, and whom
   do you miss?
And who misses you?"

But when we're dealing with questions,
perhaps it's really not what or where or who,
but *whose*. Whose are you? And whose am I?

AMAZING GRACE

"I really don't think that I'm a better person
than I was when I was twelve years old."

Words of truth and wisdom from my friend,
a man of more than seventy years,
a mellow and insightful person.
My heart speaks thanks on my behalf,
for this is my self-appraisal, too.
We may grow in openness and understanding,
be kinder, gentler, more accepting,
but never be less in need of grace
and never problem-free.

Maturity? What is it, really?
Perhaps it's this, and much, much more:
to cease expecting ease and tranquility,
to learn to navigate in sunshine, storm, and
    fog,
to know there are no hideaways where one
    escapes oneself
and leaves one's problems far behind;
to realize that no good thing is ever cheap,
that most of life is bittersweet
and comes as crisis, calling, challenge.

And most of all, maturity is this:
to see, however dimly, that problems are not
 really enemies,
but tokens of involvement and belonging
and that we don't improve with the passing
 years
but are only more and more alive to God's
 amazing grace.

I'M RIGHT HERE!

Today I heard it said
that if there were just three bees in America,
the air would be more congested with bees
than space is with stars!

Many, many nights ago
my small voice would cry out,
and father always answered,
"I'm right here. Just go to sleep."

O loving God of this space age,
you know how quickly we'd be lost in vastness
if we couldn't cry to you
and call you Father,
then hear you say,
"I'm right here. Just rest in me!"

EASTER BREAD

He walked and taught;
and as he talked
he spoke of seed,
of packaged miracle:
the seed that dies
so hungry persons may be fed.

He is that seed,
fallen into the ground
to die and rise again.
He is our Easter Bread.

BACK TO EARTH

"That's enough, now!"
Quietly, firmly, and sometimes
with suppressed exasperation,
these words have come.
I've heard them from two generations
of mothers in our family.

I've blessed the ones who've said them,
lighthouses in our homes,
providing points of reference,
unchanging sources of perspective.
Theirs was the voice of sanity and sense
in moments of rampant nonsense,
to call us back to earth,
a summons to the real.

I'M THE ONE
(To My Friends and Family)

I'm the one I never see;
my camera clicks, and they're all there
but me.

Imprisoned in myself,
I have a grandstand view
of all the faults and foibles
of everyone but me.

Perhaps I wouldn't like myself so well
if I could really see;
my thanks to all who love and like
in spite of all they see in me.

HE IS NO FOOL

"He is no fool
who gives up what he cannot keep
to gain what he cannot lose."

Noble words from the lips of James Elliot,
who died hazarding his life among the Aucas,
some of whom received the Christ
after the death of this dedicated man.

Our Lord offers no obvious bargains:
One must look long and hard,
and go deeper and deeper,
if one would see the Gift.

JOKER

My mind is landlord to my thoughts;
I invite and entertain.
But somehow vagrant thoughts move in,
and sometimes they remain.

I'm carried back
through many years of family fun
to a well-remembered joke.

We placed a birdhouse.
The day for leasing came.
The royal palace waited,
newly painted, nicely mounted,
right in size and every other way.

Proudly, haughtily, we waited:
one day, three days, ten. No birds!
They didn't like us,
the empty birdhouse seemed to say.

We peered, we gazed, we stared.
One day it came: We had a tenant!
But what? But who?
Someone, something,
looked out at us and then withdrew.
But who?

"Binoculars! Get the binoculars!" someone
 said.
And I was first in line.

I waited, waited for the movement
of the pretty little head,
that bright-eyed little songster
we wanted so to greet.

It came. I looked. I laughed!
I saw—a toad. A toad!
No silver-throated, many-colored bird.
A warty, hoarse-voiced toad.

Today I thought an inappropriate thought.
Like the toad in a birdhouse it came,
and moved in as one who planned to stay.
I shooed it, threatened it, commanded it.
I laughed at it, and thought of that joker,
the toad.

RABBI

"He stirs up the people. . . ."

They called him Rabbi. Teacher.
And he made trouble;
he caused traffic jams.

He stirred up the people,
disturbed them with revolutionary change,
and made them restless in their rest.
He ignited and excited.
He got them into his kind of trouble—
good trouble!

He still activates imaginations,
stirs stagnation, challenges corruption,
as burly truths attack proud prejudices
in the street fights of the mind.

I AM RESOLVED

I, who teach,
am resolved never to forget
that I am of the journeying people of God.
Therefore I will love answers,
but I will love questions more.
I will not seek docile acquiescence,
but suffer the creative struggle.

I will remember
that our wilderness has no terminals, only
    trails,
that truth is never a static destination
toward which I journey
and at which I arrive.
Rather, it is a horizon:
I never exhaust it,
but as I journey
I have the journeying person's great reward,
a larger world.

YOUNG IN HEART

Grandma knew this was the day,
the long-awaited and best in every year,
Christmas tree-trimming time
in the home of her small grandchild.
So that evening she telephoned across town.

The buoyant voice answered,
and eagerly teased,
"I'll bet you can't guess what we have here!"
"Could it be a Christmas tree?"
was Grandma's knowing reply.
"Uh huh. Do you want to talk to it?"

Talking trees or talked-to trees,
it's all the same when one is young in heart.
Treasure the child within you and around you:
the free imagination and blithe spirit.
They warm the winter nights of memory.

STEP BACK

"You won't see the cathedral
if you hold your nose up to one stone."

I once said this in my classes,
and those words come tumbling back
on me today.

One needs perspective to view magnificence;
the greater the scene, the more distance one
　requires.

God is in the cathedral business;
his cathedrals are you and I.
In our impatience we may sometimes
choose a self who isn't the one he intends.

We lose ourselves.

If we would rediscover,
we must step back, walk and talk with God,
and think with him.
It is his plan.

WISE LOVE

"I guess one has to tie them in
a little—but with a band of love,
not with barbed wire."
Graphic words of a wise and loving woman
as she reflected on her role as mother.

Yes, let there be gold in your discipline,
the gold of love; and let it sparkle,
that it may be unmistakable and readily
   recognizable.
Leave no room for vindictiveness or
   vengeance,
for barbed and bloody laceration,
because discipline becomes the stuff of
   memory
to recall us homeward or drive us far away.

WE NEED EACH OTHER

How quickly they grow up!
A baby only yesterday,
and now she's tall as her mother
(in heels, you know), almost fifteen.

The daily news reported a violent holdup,
with one man killed outright,
on the very corner where she and her friends
must walk on their daily errands.
I told her of it, and, to urge more care,
I warned, "It's a bad world, my dear."
Instantly she responded, "Not all of it!"
"That's true," I replied;
"we must keep reminding one another."
Smiling, she answered, "But I was
the one who remembered."

I felt taught.

We need each other.
The young need us who are older
to help them grow up,
and we need their buoyant spirits
to help us remember the beauty of our world.

I SLAMMED THE DOOR

Today
I judged them,
my sister and my brother.

I slammed the door on them;
I played God,
climbed onto his throne.

I was unqualified.

I shamed God's saving grace,
forgot that judgment
is his alone.

I judged,
a greater wrong than any sin
I might presume to judge.
Dear God, forgive.

SOME DAY WE'LL SEE

God has no grown-up children here,
but toddlers all, falling, stumbling,
picked up to try again,
tripping over many things
that make them fall,
but mostly just over their own two feet.

Some day we'll see
that this spinning world
is one vast day-care center,

God's kindergarten, our home
away from Home.

THE FIRST BOOK

There he sat in the grocery cart,
the all-pro in his family,
wearing a white number twelve
on the bright blue football jersey,
waiting with his mother in the checkout line.

Tentatively, curiously, objectively
he looked us over—me, my wife, our
    daughter—
as we stood there smiling,
freely enjoying and taking our time exposure.

One long moment of dignified deliberation,
and suddenly that "tiny two" smiled the
    smiliest smile.
"He's reading his first book," I said,
"our grown-up faces, and now he feels
it's safe to smile."

Of all the children's books,
the first and most important are the faces—
family faces, neighborhood faces, community
    faces,
each with its mood and its story.

They read us, these clear-eyed ones,
read acceptance or rejection, serenity or
   anxiety,
attentiveness or indifference, happiness or
   misery—
all these, and much, much more.

One question looms for me: What kind of
   book
is my face?

THE HALO TILTS

As I have seen
the human situation,
there's much that calls for
mellow laughter.

Isn't it true?
We over-correct and over-kill.
We don't really walk; we lurch.

We don't make a thing right
without making it so right-right
it's wrong again.

The halo tilts.

FORGET-ME-NOT

A dreaded day—
scary, the children would say.
I had two errands, both crucial and painful—
a day to run away from.

I wished I had stayed in bed.

Then they came,
two memos from heaven,
red streaks across the window scene:
Mr. and Mrs. Cardinal,
just passing by.

The briefest glimpse—
two birds,
God's flaming forget-me-nots—
but enough to remind me
of the Big Hand that holds
all days.

JUST THINK

The big examination was over
in the sixth-grade civics class.
That night she added this to her
usual bedtime prayer: "And please, God,
make Omaha the capital of Nebraska.
 Amen."

But think, my child, just think:
If God would send a state house
winging on one child's troubled prayer,
and change your grade from B to A—
yes, if God placed us in a world like that—
think of all the frightened people
in the state house, and all the perfect papers,
unemployed teachers, confused preachers,
stationary rivers, tropical shivers,
and the infinite magic mess!

THE QUESTION

I remember Mama.
I'm thinking of her later years.

With each of our visits
she'd wait with her special question
until everyone was settled, all the welcoming
   done,
and the children well content.

Then she'd settle herself to listen,
and it would surely come, that all-important
   question
she'd hungered so to ask.

Peering intently into my face, she'd inquire,
"And Gerhard, how *are* you?"

And she had time for the answer.

Noble question, affirming, healing, human,
cruel only when one doesn't really care.
And have you noticed? There's no short
   answer.

BE READY

"Be prepared," they told us
when we were very young.
"One must always be ready for death.
We live in the valley of the shadow;
don't be taken by surprise!"

They meant to teach us well.

But what of the other half?
"Be prepared for *life*.
At any moment it may assault you.
Be ready for the sudden storms of truth.
Listen for the thunder, and watch for the
  lightning
that plays along the horizons of your life.
Be ready for the crashing break-in
of an overpowering meaning or an all-
  consuming love.
Our enemy, death, broods and hovers, 'tis
  true,
but over all towers our taller friend.
He awaits his moment, too.
Expect to be surprised;
there's always new welcoming to do."

WELL TAUGHT

She biked past us in full speed,
her blonde curls flying in the wind,
as we walked leisurely together, my wife and
 I.
I would guess that she was seven.

We sensed her bid for our attention
when, turning the corner,
she sped back, directly toward us.
Everything about her seemed to say,
"Now, what do you think of *this*?"

My wife rose to the occasion with the cheery
 comment,
"You surely handle your bike well, don't you?"
The response was instant and sincere: "I
 know!"

We looked at each other,
laughing as she sped away,
for we knew we'd had a lesson
in how to receive that special gift of
 affirmation,
a compliment.
I think how awkward and embarrassed,
how ill at ease and insincere we often are
when someone speaks kind words.
But now, well taught by our young teacher,
we know the honest thing to do.

LOOK AGAIN

"I'm of the old school,
and I'm against it!"

She said it with a toss
of her proud gray head,
and I knew the discussion was over.

I wanted to say,
"But, friend, you forget.
School isn't out yet.
Living is learning,
and learning is living.
It's sad to see you hunker down
and burrow in
like a frightened little rabbit.
Our world is in trouble.
The good old days
weren't good enough,
and now we must rethink
what we've thought,
reevaluate what we've treasured,
re-view what we've accepted as true.
Look again at all you've looked at;
there's more to be and become."

THE MEETING

I met a man this wintry morning.
Stooping to pull on my overshoes,
I looked up, and there he was.

I greeted him with a hello;
he greeted me as pleasantly,
but hello was all he said.

That is all;
hardly worth the telling
in this world of large events,
and yet enough to call forth the question in
  me,
"What do I really know of this young man?

"I've never known his name,
his date or place of birth,
his family, friends, or home address.
I can't guess what's on his mind or in his
  heart,
or where he's been or where he's going.
And yet, I know he's born and didn't ask to be;
and he will die, but doesn't want to."

I know, too, with knowledge born of faith,
that he is loved and wanted here on earth
and in the highest heaven.

One thing more I know:
He is lonely.
Like me, he knows much more than he can
  tell,
has feelings he cannot fully share.

These universals bind us all together;
we share the wonder and the pain of being;
we know its source and sense a Presence.
Essentially, we do know one another.

NOW I THINK I KNOW

What makes me who I am?
Time was when I couldn't have answered,
but now I think I know.

Not only once-for-all occasions, spectacular
 sensations,
but mostly hidden, silent constants.

This is the secret
of the very continent beneath me,
molded not only by earthquakes and
 eruptions,
explosions and convulsions,
but mainly by the ongoing and repeated
drippings, flowings, freezings, thawings,
 burnings, blowings,
crushings, grindings, and erodings—
unpublished repetitions.

So toils God's Spirit in me as renewing power,
consuming fire, and healing balm.
He acts in my continuing petitions,
 confessions,
doxologies, intercessions, countless Our
 Fathers,
and endless Amens.

He makes me who I am.

GROUNDS FOR HOPE

"The light shines in the darkness,
and the darkness has not overcome it."

If I am asked
what are my grounds for hope,
this is my answer.

Light is lord over darkness,
truth is lord over falsehood,
life is ever lord over death.

Of all the facts I daily live with,
there's none more comforting
than this: If I have two rooms,
one dark, the other light,
and I open the door between them,
the dark room becomes lighter
without the light one
becoming darker. I know
this is no headline,
but it's a marvelous footnote;
and God comforts me in that.

HE NEVER LOSES TOUCH

"Salvation belongs to our God
who sits upon the throne. . . .
and God will wipe away every tear
from their eyes. . . ."

What a leap from God's throne to my tears!
It almost takes my breath away.

Can it be that he who claims
"blessing and glory . . . and honor
and power and might"
has stooped to me
and listened to my faintest cry?

Other rulers,
blinded by the glare of power,
forget.

To think that God inhabits
my most tear-blinded day,
knows every empty dish
and fevered mind and heavy heart!
He never loses touch!

SOMETHING BEAUTIFUL

He is anonymous, though not forgotten,
for he rode into my life and out again,
leaving me something beautiful.

It was a hot summer evening in eastern Montana;
I'd just washed my car in Porcupine Creek,
a hidden little stream, far from village or ranch.
With darkness approaching, I hurriedly started my car
and mired it down in the sand.

I scanned the horizon and tried not to panic,
but suddenly there was just desolation,
no beauty at all, as I helplessly, ruefully
called myself many kinds of fool.

Then he came, this storybook man,
galloping toward me out of the west.
"Small comfort," I thought, "one man on a horse!"

With very few words, but boundless goodwill,
he quickly unfurled his lasso and secured it.
"Start your car," was his cheerful command,
"and turn the wheels slowly. Slowly.
Remember, easy does it!"
I did as commanded, and to my amazement
that sturdy young horse flattened his belly
almost to the ground, dug in as though he enjoyed it,
and with one mighty tug pulled me out of the mud!

More quickly than I can recount it
this man of few words interrupted my thank-
　yous
and offers to pay, turned his horse westward,
and galloped away with a wave of his hand.
So now I'm in debt to whoever needs me;
I've been given a gift,
something bright and beautiful,
to pass on.

WE NEED EXITS

I heard a lecture today:
no exits, all freeway;
no urge to reflection;
no time for gestation.
How I longed for a path
or a meadow to roam in!

We need freeways,
thruways to knowledge.
But we need exits, too:
side roads of intimacy,
experiences of humanity—
our own and that of others.

We need to stay close enough
to see doors ajar and tasks unfinished,
babies, unweathered and new,
aged ones, seasoned and tired,

celebrations in progress,
and processions
to "the silent city on the hill."

Lectures without pulse and breath
leave it all in the book.

TO BE CONTINUED

The subject was counseling,
for we were colleagues in the task.

We spoke of how often students
crave concrete examples of success.
One among us recounted a most recent
   request:
"Please tell us about some of your failures!"
The teacher's reply surprised them all:
"I really don't think I've had any failures."

In explanation he added,
"When one works with persons
the story is 'to be continued';
we never see the end where God is at work.
The evidence is never in,
so when we're doing our best,
our greatest work is to get out of God's way."

I've thought, what mellow compassion and
   wisdom,
what comfort in a world that likes to count
and measure and weigh!

HELP US TO LET GO

I forgot my glasses today,
left them at the home of a friend;
went to get them and forgot my hat;
went to get the hat, and on the way
met an acquaintance of many years,
remembered the face, but forgot the name.
I looked for an excuse.
"I'm old!" I said, "old, old, old!"
And I was angry
and sad.
Then I remembered
some things I'd forgotten I knew:

Forgetfulness is a gift,
one of the best of our gift-giving God.
Without it, what would we do?
We couldn't travel this day's journey;
we'd be crushed by the burden of the past,
broken under the unbearable load.

So, dear God, guide us in our forgetting;
help us to let go;
make us ready to relinquish
the painful baggage of yesterday—
the slurs and slaps, the burns and bruises.
School us in purposeful forgetting
as we grow old.

THANK YOU

Dear God,
I'm sorry!
I really am.
That's all I have to say today;
you understand.
Thank you. Amen.

MY PERSONAL DEVIL

I've noticed
that my personal devil
is passionately in favor of the good
as long as it keeps me from the Best.
He never deals in blacks and whites,
but loves the many shades of gray;
he likes options, and offers many.
He keeps the lines blurred.

His art is to distract.

FIVE SAD WORDS

When I think of what the passing years can
   do,
have done, to many a teacher,
I'm frightened by five fearsome words:
They learn to look away.

These tell the stark and dreary story
of the late-blooming child,
ego-starved, fed often on the husks of failure,
seldom tasting sweet success;
of calloused and discouraged teachers,
withholding life-supporting words and
   gestures,
allowing silence and indifference
to speak their judgment and contempt.

They learn to look away.
Five sad words;
they mustn't be true
of me, of you!

THE LONELIEST MOMENT

It happened one September morning
on a street in the Big Apple;
I shouldn't have been walking there.

With hardly a sound he came,
leaped across my path from nowhere
and pressed a long-bladed knife against my
 side.
His voice a whispered snarl:
"I want your money—all of it!"
With practiced stealth he robbed me
of my watch and all my cash.
I'll not forget the hostility in his eyes;
it was my loneliest moment.

But there have been other moments
when Truth has come at me
"from behind and in the night,"
when the long, sharp blade of fact
has blocked my path, leaving me no exit,
and stripping me of my pride.

The difference was in the face.
Truth is not foe, but friend who comes
stealthily finding, capturing,
loving me into painful change,
stretching me in that lonely moment
into a larger becoming.

WHAT WASTE!

"If I could do it over again,
I'd laugh and cry less at TV
and more at real life."

I heard these words this morning;
they speak impressively to me.

What waste of God-born energies
to let oneself be wrung dry
by the fictitious and the superficial
and make oneself indifferent
to authentic comedy and real tragedy!

WISTFUL

I experience my brokenness in this,
that I am wistful
before the innocence
of a child.

TWO WORDS

Two words I'd leave
to those who are coming after:
Expect more!

Expect to see more light
in what you've understood;
more beauty in all
you still admire;
more truth in all
you've long believed;
more goodness in all
you've learned to love.

THE TALKING MONTH

Tonight our home is filled with flowers,
six exquisite bouquets.
No anniversary, holiday, wedding, birthday,
or any special day. Just flowers!

Why? I seem to hear you ask.
The reason—poignant, painful, unequivocal:
October 29, and tonight a killing freeze, they
   say.
This is our autumn rescue mission!

October, the talking month,
speaking the soundless language of mortality:
"The way to love a thing
is to know that it can be lost."

MY UNTRUSTING HEART

I stood outside her bedroom door,
eavesdropping as she continued
the prayers we'd just been praying.
"God besh the whole forld!"
("God bless the whole world!")
I heard her say.
Yes, I thought to myself,
the smaller we are, the less we seem to fear
the sweeping statement, the expansive
   promise,
and exuberant response.

Today I'm captive to my cautious prayers,
my shackled mind, my grown-up heart.
I need her for my freedom, and for courage
to receive this vast and frightening world,
and for looking deep into the dark abyss
of my untrusting heart, more frightening still.

PETE

Pete died today,
and now as I look up
I see a patch of blue against the sky
over God's vast forest of humankind.

A great oak has fallen—
no, rather, risen, been harvested
by the Master Woodsman's loving hand.
We miss it;
the future shows a different face.

Storyteller, picture-maker,
child of God,
no strident voice was Pete's,
or overbearing, self-promoting,
but patient, trustful, kind.

HE TAKES COMMAND

"Jesus also was invited."

They planned a common wedding
but invited a most uncommon guest,
and things got out of hand.

Because Jesus came
we're talking still,
recalling the Big Surprise.

It's always so with Jesus:
He overfills the moment.
Invite him, and you've thrown the door ajar
to the impossible,
and things get out of hand— your hand.
He takes command.

I'M NOT SUPER

I'm not super—
not a super husband,
or a super father,
brother, friend.

No, I'm not super,
but I don't have to be,
so now I can be free.

No, no, I'm not a super person;
I mustn't try to be,
for then I'm proud;
I'm brittle, hard, unyielding,
not strong at all, but weak.
I'm not a super anyone,
but I've a super God.
He sees me as a somebody,
and that's super!

HOME ROAD

They taught me well
when I was very young,
took my small hand and led me
on the Old Road.

They told me of my God,
his mighty works and caring ways,
all that he's done, is doing, and will do.
They said, "This is the Home Road,
and home roads never change."

I believed them, and went my way.

Years flew.
I journeyed far,
and then returned one day.

Expecting faces to have changed,
I counted on some things to be the same:
Roads, I thought, the roads will be the same!
But, no, it wasn't true,
not true that home roads never change.

Bulldozers had done their ruthless work:
fence lines torn away,
curves and corners straightened—
everything arranged and rearranged
for greater speeds on mechanical steeds.

I felt the shock of change,
when suddenly one thought steadied me:
"North is still north," I told myself,
"and south still south. The Big Dipper
holds its place!"

Roads are more than sculpted earth
for feet to feel and eyes to see;
they're highways for the heart and soul,
for faith-prints pointing toward one's Home.
So let the changes come.

THOSE STRONG FEET

"I fled Him, down the nights and down the
  days;
I fled Him down the arches of the years. . . .
I hid from Him, . . . from those strong feet
that followed, followed after. . ." (Francis
  Thompson).

We are the questing ones, we say,
searching, groping for our God.
But would that we could know ourselves as he
  knows us—
fugitives, escapees, rebels,
the wanted ones, the longed-for ones.

God is the questing one, the gaunt and
  tireless one;
he calls and sends us to one another
to speak the wooing Word, the Name,
to break each habit of ingenious evasion,
and gently block all exits
from chastening love,
to listen for each footfall of those strong feet
that even now follow, follow after.